ASTEROIDS AND COMETS

SPACE-THEMED RECIPES

by Jane Yates

Minneapolis, Minnesota

Credits

Cover and title page, © 24K-Production/Adobe Stock and © Olga Popova/Shutterstock and © Natthapol Siridech/Shutterstock; 5 top left, DestinaDesign/Shutterstock.com; 5 right middle, Christos Georghiou/Shutterstock.com; 6 bottom right, NASA/JPL-Caltech/ASU/Peter Rubin/Public Domain; 8 bottom left, ESA/Rosetta/MPS for OSIRIS Team MPS/UPD/LAM/IAA/SSO/INTA/UPM/DASP/IDA/ ©ESA; 8 botttom right, NASA/Public Domain; 18 bottom right, NASA/W. Liller/Public Domain; 22 top right, NASA/Public Domain; all other photos ©Austen Photography

Bearport Publishing Company Product Development Team

Publisher: Jen Jenson; Director of Product Development: Spencer Brinker; Editorial Director: Allison Juda; Editor: Cole Nelson; Editor: Tiana Tran; Production Editor: Naomi Reich; Art Director: Kim Jones; Designer: Kayla Eggert; Designer: Steve Scheluchin; Production Specialist: Owen Hamlin

Statement on Usage of Generative Artificial Intelligence

Bearport Publishing remains committed to publishing high-quality nonfiction books. Therefore, we restrict the use of generative AI to ensure accuracy of all text and visual components pertaining to a book's subject. See BearportPublishing.com for details.

Produced for Bearport Publishing by BlueAppleWorks Inc.

Managing Editor for BlueAppleWorks: Melissa McClellan
Art Director: T.J. Choleva
Photo Research: Jane Reid

Library of Congress Cataloging-in-Publication Data

Names: Yates, Jane author
Title: Asteroids and comets : space-themed recipes / by Jane Yates.
Description: Minneapolis, Minnesota : Bearport Publishing Company, [2026] |
   Series: Space-licious! Out-of-this-world recipes | Includes
   bibliographical references and index.
Identifiers: LCCN 2025001538 (print) | LCCN 2025001539 (ebook) | ISBN
   9798895770306 library binding | ISBN 9798895771471 ebook
Subjects: LCSH: Cooking--Juvenile literature |
   Asteroids--Miscellanea--Juvenile literature |
   Comets--Miscellanea--Juvenile literature | Outer
   space--Miscellanea--Juvenile literature | LCGFT: Cookbooks
Classification: LCC TX652.5 .Y374 2026 (print) | LCC TX652.5 (ebook) |
   DDC 641.5/686--dc23/eng/20250227
LC record available at https://lccn.loc.gov/2025001538
LC ebook record available at https://lccn.loc.gov/2025001539

Copyright © 2026 Bearport Publishing Company. All rights reserved. No part of this publication may be reproduced in whole or in part, stored in any retrieval system, or transmitted in any form or by any means, electronic, mechanical, photocopying, recording, or otherwise, without written permission from the publisher. Bearport Publishing is a division of FlutterBee Education Group.

For more information, write to Bearport Publishing, 3500 American Blvd W, Suite 150, Bloomington, MN 55431.

CONTENTS

Space-licious! 4

Cheese Blast Asteroids 6

Crispy Comets 8

Chocolate Space Rocks 12

Potato Asteroid Belt 14

Asteroid Punch 16

Comet Cupcakes 18

Meet a Hungry Astronaut 22
Glossary 23
Index 24
Read More 24
Learn More Online 24
About the Author 24

SPACE-LICIOUS!

Let's learn about space and cooking at the same time! How would you like to try some cheese asteroids or chocolate space rocks? With this book, you can make six delicious, out-of-this-world recipes. Let's blast off!

Measuring liquid ingredients

- Use a measuring cup with a spout. This makes it easier to pour the liquids without spilling.
- Always set the measuring cup on a flat surface.
- When adding liquid, bend down so your eye is level with the measurements on the cup. This ensures you have the right amount.

Measuring dry ingredients

- Scoop the ingredients with the correct size measuring cup or measuring spoon.
- Level off the top with the back of a butter knife or another straight edge. This will ensure you have an accurate amount.

Ingredients

Most of these recipes can be made with things you probably already have in your kitchen. Before you start each recipe, make sure you have all the ingredients you need. It's a good idea to set everything on the counter before you begin.

Microwave safety

Each microwave works a little differently, so ask an adult to help show you how to use yours. Be sure to use only dishes that are safe for the microwave, such as glass or ceramic. Never use metal or aluminum foil in the microwave. After cooking, carefully check that a dish isn't too hot before taking it out.

Allergy Alert!

Recipes that include common allergens, such as wheat, tree nuts, peanuts, eggs, or dairy, are marked with a special symbol. Please use a safe **substitute** ingredient if you need to.

 Wheat   Eggs

 Dairy   Peanuts

 Tree nuts

 Always ask for an adult's help with knives and when using the oven or stove.

CHEESE BLAST ASTEROIDS

Asteroids are rocky space objects that **orbit** the sun between Mars and Jupiter. They come in lots of shapes and sizes, but many are **spherical**. Have a blast making some cheesy asteroids as a delicious snack!

Ingredients

- An 8-oz. (226-g) package of cream cheese, softened at room temperature
- 1 cup shredded cheddar cheese, plus extra for topping
- ¼ cup corn chips
- ¼ cup shelled walnut pieces
- ¼ cup dried cranberries
- Star-shaped crackers (optional)

Equipment

- A mixing spoon
- A medium-sized mixing bowl
- 3 small bowls
- A plate

Allergy Alert!

Most asteroids are made of rocks, but scientists think some are made of metal.

1. Use a spoon to scrape all the softened cream cheese into a medium-sized mixing bowl.

2. Next, add the shredded cheddar cheese to the bowl and mix together with a spoon. Set aside.

3. Put the corn chips into a small bowl, and break them up with your hands. Place the walnuts into another small bowl and break apart any big pieces. Add the dried cranberries to a third small bowl.

4. To make the sun, scoop up a large portion of the cheese mixture and roll it into a ball with your hands. Place it in the center of a plate, and flatten it. Sprinkle with extra cheddar cheese.

5. For the asteroids, roll five or six smaller balls in the bowls of toppings. Be sure to make at least one of each! Place the cheesy asteroids on the plate around the sun. If you want, add star-shaped crackers for space-themed decoration!

7

CRISPY COMETS

Comets are big objects made of ice, rocks, and dust. They travel through space in large **elliptical** orbits around the sun. When they get close to the sun, comets glow and form long tails made of dust and gases that can stretch millions of miles. These crispy chickpea patties look like comets, and their **condiments** stretch behind them like tails.

Ingredients

- A 16-oz. (454-g) can chickpeas
- 3 Tbsp all-purpose flour
- 1 tsp kosher salt
- 1 tsp garlic powder
- 1 tsp cumin
- 1 tsp paprika
- ¼ cup Greek yogurt, plus more for serving
- 1 Tbsp olive oil
- Hummus, or other condiment

Allergy Alert!

Comets have rocky, icy surfaces. Their tails form when their orbits are nearer to the sun.

8

Equipment

* A strainer
* A medium bowl
* A large mixing bowl
* A potato masher or a fork
* A small bowl
* Spoons
* A baking sheet
* A spatula
* Plates for serving

1. Empty the can of chickpeas into a strainer and rinse with cold water. Set the strainer over a medium bowl to drain for 5 or 10 minutes.

2. Put the drained chickpeas into a large bowl. Mash them with a potato masher or fork. It's okay if there are some chunks left, but there shouldn't be any whole chickpeas.

3. Add the flour to the bowl with the mashed chickpeas.

4 Add all the spices together into a small bowl. Stir with a spoon until mixed.

5 Add ¼ cup of the yogurt and all of the spices to the bowl with the flour and mashed chickpeas. Mix everything together with a spoon.

6 Spread the olive oil evenly on a baking sheet. Then, scoop out about ¼ cup of the mixture at a time and place on the baking sheet. You should have six portions.

10

7 Flatten the chickpea balls into patties using the back of a spoon.

8 With an adult's help, **preheat** your oven to 400°F (205°C). Once the oven is ready, bake the patties for 15 minutes. Then, have an adult use a spatula to flip them over and put them back in the oven for another 15 minutes.

9 To serve, add spoonfuls of hummus to a plate and use the tip of the spoon to shape them into long tails. Place a chickpea comet at the head of each tail and spread some Greek yogurt over it. Now, your glowing comets are ready to eat!

CHOCOLATE SPACE ROCKS

Space *rocks*! But what are space rocks? These objects are bits of floating **debris** from comets, asteroids, moons, and even planets. The rocks are sometimes made of the same minerals that are found on Earth. Since chocolate has minerals too, you can make these yummy snacks and pretend you're eating space rocks!

Ingredients

* 2 cups crispy puffed rice cereal
* 1 cup semi-sweet chocolate chips
* 1 Tbsp honey
* ½ cup peanut butter or butterscotch chips
* Sprinkles for decoration

Allergy Alert!

Equipment

* A baking sheet
* Parchment paper
* A large mixing bowl
* A small microwave-safe bowl
* A mixing spoon
* A soup spoon

12

1. Line a baking sheet with parchment paper and set aside.

2. Add the cereal to a large bowl.

3. Put the chocolate chips in a small microwave-safe bowl and heat in the microwave for 30 seconds. Stir the chocolate with a spoon. Repeat heating for 30 seconds, stirring in between, until the chocolate is almost melted. Then, stir until the chocolate is completely smooth.

4. Add the honey to the melted chocolate and stir until well combined.

5. Pour the chocolate mixture over the cereal, scraping the bowl with a spoon. Add the peanut butter or butterscotch chips and stir until the crispy rice is fully coated with chocolate.

6. Use a soup spoon to scoop up the cereal mixture and place it in small piles on the prepared baking sheet. The rocky piles can be different shapes. Decorate with sprinkles and chill in the fridge for 30 minutes. Enjoy!

POTATO ASTEROID BELT

Most asteroids orbit the sun in the area of space between Jupiter and Mars. This is known as the asteroid belt, and it contains millions of asteroids of different shapes and sizes. You can make your own asteroid belt out of these tasty smashed potatoes.

Ingredients

- 9 to 12 small potatoes, washed
- 1 Tbsp olive oil
- Salt and pepper
- Chipotle mustard or other condiment of your choice

Equipment

- A saucepan
- A strainer
- A baking sheet
- A small bowl
- A spatula
- A serving plate

1. Place the potatoes in a saucepan and fill with enough cold water to cover the potatoes by about 1 in. (2.5 cm). Ask an adult to boil the potatoes until soft, about 15 to 20 minutes. Ask the adult to then drain the potatoes and let them cool. While they do, preheat the oven to 400°F (205°C).

2. Spread olive oil on a baking sheet to cover its surface.

3. Arrange the potatoes evenly on the baking sheet. Then, use the bottom of a small bowl to gently smash each potato.

4. Sprinkle each potato asteroid with salt and pepper.

5. With an adult's help, bake the potatoes in the oven. After 15 minutes, have an adult flip them over using a spatula. Continue baking until golden and crispy, about 10 to 20 more minutes.

6. Allow the potatoes to cool. Decorate a plate with a swirl of chipotle mustard or other condiment. Then, place the potato asteroids in a circle around the plate.

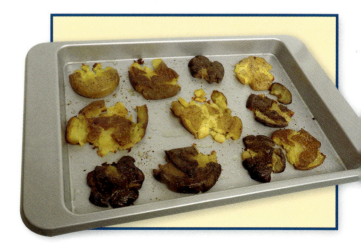

15

ASTEROID PUNCH

Asteroids orbit the sun from more than 200 million miles (322 million km) away. But you can make this yummy asteroid punch in a bowl at home. With a gentle stir, watch your melon asteroids slowly orbit around an orange-slice sun.

Ingredients

- ½ small watermelon
- ½ cantaloupe with seeds scraped out
- 1 can frozen pink lemonade concentrate
- A 10-oz. (300-mL) bottle of ginger ale
- An orange slice

Equipment

- A melon baller
- 2 large bowls
- A spoon
- A ladle
- A serving glass
- A reusable straw

BE SAFE! NOTE: Be sure to ask an adult to cut the fruit!

1. Use a melon baller to scoop out balls of watermelon and cantaloupe, and add them to a large bowl.

2. Empty the can of frozen lemonade into a second large bowl. Then, using the same can as a measuring device, add two more cans full of water to the bowl. Stir with a spoon until the frozen concentrate is **dissolved**. Next, add the ginger ale to the bowl.

3. Carefully add the melon asteroids to the punch.

4. Place the orange slice in the center of the melon asteroids. When you stir gently, the asteroids will circle the sun!

5. Use a ladle to fill a glass with punch, and add a reusable straw.

COMET CUPCAKES

In the past, some people who saw comets believed they were signs of bad luck. Today, we know that comets come from the early formation of our solar system. Celebrate these amazing space objects with some colorful and tasty cupcakes!

Ingredients

For the Cupcakes:
- ⅓ cup white sugar
- ⅔ cup all-purpose flour
- ½ tsp baking powder
- ¼ tsp baking soda
- A pinch of salt
- 1 large egg
- 3 Tbsp vegetable oil
- ¼ cup milk
- ½ tsp vanilla extract
- Assorted candies and sprinkles

For the Icing:
- ½ cup butter or margarine, softened
- About 1 cup powdered sugar
- 1 Tbsp milk
- 1 tsp vanilla extract
- Food coloring

Allergy Alert!

Halley's comet is visible from Earth every 75 to 80 years. It will next appear in the year 2061.

18

Equipment

- A muffin pan
- 6 cupcake liners
- 2 mixing bowls
- A mixing spoon
- A wooden toothpick
- A butter knife

Cupcakes

1. Have an adult preheat the oven to 350°F (175°C). While they do, line a muffin pan with cupcake liners and set it aside.

2. Add the sugar, flour, baking powder, and baking soda to a large mixing bowl. Add a pinch of salt and mix with a spoon.

3. Next, add the egg, oil, milk, and vanilla extract to the dry ingredients. Stir with a spoon until well mixed.

4. Spoon the mixture into the cupcake liners, filling them about two-thirds full.

5. With an adult's help, bake the cupcakes in the oven for 20 minutes or until a toothpick inserted into the center comes out clean. Let the cupcakes cool completely while you prepare the icing.

Icing

1 Beat the softened butter or margarine for about a minute using a spoon. If you prefer, you can use a hand mixer with an adult's help.

2 Add 1 cup of powdered sugar, a little at a time, stirring well after each addition.

3 Add the milk and vanilla extract. Stir until well mixed.

4 Add a few drops of food coloring to the icing and stir. Repeat until you have the desired color.

NOTE: If your icing is too thick, add several drops of milk, and stir well. If it's too thin, add a spoonful of powdered sugar, and mix well.

5 Put a **dollop** of icing onto each cupcake.

6 Use a butter knife to spread the icing evenly.

7 Use assorted candies and sprinkles to make comet shapes on each cupcake.

MEET A HUNGRY ASTRONAUT

Jessica Meir is a biologist and astronaut. During one mission to space, she spent seven months on the International Space Station doing **experiments** on ways to grow lettuce in space. Meir believes that everything is more fun when you're floating, including making one of her favorite foods—a **charcuterie** board!

Meir eating greens she grew in space

Make a Charcuterie Board

1. Use a cookie cutter to cut out star shapes from slices of cheddar cheese.

2. Carefully slice a few pieces of a ready-to-eat sausage or use round circles of lunch meat.

3. Ask an adult to help make carrot ribbons using a vegetable peeler.

4. Arrange the cheese stars, meat, carrot ribbons, and some star-shaped crackers on a tray to create a space-licious charcuterie board.

GLOSSARY

charcuterie an assembly of meats and cheeses

condiments seasonings, sauces, or toppings added after food is prepared

debris scattered pieces of something broken or destroyed

dissolved a solid having become fully mixed into a liquid

dollop a small amount of soft food

elliptical shaped in an oval a bit like a flattened circle

experiments scientific tests performed to try to find out if an idea is true

orbit the path an object takes as it moves around the sun or a planet

preheat to heat in advance to a set temperature

spherical having a three-dimensional, mostly round shape

substitute a similar item used in place of another item

INDEX

allergy 5–6, 8, 12, 18
asteroid belt 14
cheese 4, 6–7, 22
chickpeas 8–11
chocolate 4, 12–13
cupcakes 18–19, 21
debris 12
Halley's comet 18
Meir, Jessica 22
orbit 6, 8, 14, 16
potatoes 14–15
punch 16–17

READ MORE

Betts, Bruce. *Asteroids and Comets: Orbiting Space Rocks (Exploring Our Solar System With the Planetary Society).* Minneapolis: Lerner Publications, 2025.

Mather, Charis. *Asteroids and Comets: Top Secret Data (Space Files).* Minneapolis: Bearport Publishing, 2024.

LEARN MORE ONLINE

1. Go to **FactSurfer.com** or scan the QR code below.

2. Enter "**Asteroid and Comet Recipes**" into the search box.

3. Click on the cover of this book to see a list of websites.

ABOUT THE AUTHOR

Jane Yates is an avid cook who worked in restaurants while attending art school. She has written more than 20 craft books for children.